AF227491

RICH KINGDOM, POOR AMBASSADORS

Something Is Not Right. Now You Hold the Cure

Dr. Jean Héder Petit-Frère

Copyright © 2026 by Dr. Jean Héder Petit-Frère

All rights reserved.

No part of this book may be reproduced, stored in a retrieval system, or transmitted in any form or by any means electronic, mechanical, photocopying, recording, or otherwise without the prior written permission of the publisher, except for brief quotations in reviews or scholarly works.

Scripture References

Unless otherwise indicated, Scripture quotations are taken from the Holy Bible, New International Version (NIV).

Other translations used include the New King James Version (NKJV), English Standard Version (ESV), and Amplified Bible (AMP).

Published by

Kingdom Records Unlimited

ISBN: 978-1-971611-40-2

www.jhpetitfrere.com

Printed in the United States of America

Dedication

This book is dedicated to every believer who loves God deeply, yet has lived under quiet financial pressure, silent fear, or unspoken anxiety.

To the sons and daughters who were taught how to serve, but never taught how to rest.

To those who gave faithfully, prayed sincerely, and still wondered why peace felt elusive.

This work is for the ambassadors who sensed that something was not right, not because the Kingdom is lacking, but because alignment was missing.

May these pages restore clarity, heal trust, and reposition you in the river where provision flows naturally from the care of a faithful Father.

A rich King deserves confident ambassadors. This is your invitation to live as one.

Acknowledgment

No significant work ever gets done in isolation.

While this book carries my name, it is the fruit of relationships, conversations, corrections, prayers, and shared adventures that have formed both the message and the messenger.

First of all, I praise God, my Father, the true source of all wisdom, provision, and revelation. This book is not solely the product of human intellect; rather, it is the result of moments of clarity, correction, and alignment under His guidance. Glory be to him.

To my wife, Marcia Elaine Petit-Frère, thank you for your patience, your strength, and your quiet constancy. You have walked with me through seasons of faith, hardship, and progress, and your presence has been both anchor and mirror. I salute you.

To my children, I appreciate your love, your understanding, and your willingness to engage on a path that has so frequently required sacrifice. I hope this message is not only taught but also lived out, allowing you to fully embrace what God has prepared for you.

Your appetite for truth has honed this message for the sons and daughters of this vision throughout nations connected to leaders who have listened, questioned, wrestled, and matured. Genuine conversations, real struggles, and real lives gave birth to many of the thoughts in this book.

To our partners, friends, and supporters who have stood with the ministry throughout the years, thank you for your faithfulness. Because of you, we have been able to continue advancing the work of the Kingdom. Thank you for your generosity and confidence.

Thank you to the wider body of Christ, near and distant, whose teachings, writings, and examples have helped my own knowledge. We all stand on the shoulders of others, and I am thankful for every voice that has pointed me back to truth.

And last, to you, the reader, thank you for your desire to interact, to ponder, and to realign. You must live out this book in your life before it is complete.

May what is stated here bring not only understanding but also transformation.

Author's Note

This book was not written to provoke controversy. It was written to restore order.

For years, I have watched sincere believers struggling not because they lacked faith, discipline, or generosity, but because they were never taught how to live from the center of the Kingdom rather than from the pressure of circumstances.

I have heard the verse, "Seek first the Kingdom of God," quoted countless times. What I have heard far less is someone patiently teaching people how to do that, especially in the area of finances.

This book is not a reaction to prosperity extremes, nor is it a defense of poverty theology. It is an invitation to something far more stable and biblical: presence-centered Kingdom living.

I did not write this as a theoretician. I wrote it as a pastor, a father, a steward, and a fellow learner, one who has walked through provision and pressure, abundance and lack, clarity and correction.

What you will read here is not a formula. It is a realignment.

If at any point these pages confront you, let them. If they comfort you, receive it. If they correct you, welcome the freedom that comes with truth.

My prayer is simple: that you would leave fear behind, restore God as your source, and discover the peace of living fully in the river of His Kingdom.

Foreword

Some books inform.

Some books inspire.

And then, some books realign.

Rich Kingdom, Poor Ambassadors belongs to the latter.

For years, the Church has wrestled often uncomfortably with the subject of money. On one side, we have seen excess, manipulation, and distortion; on the other, silence, fear, and resignation. What has been missing is not Scripture, but order.

Dr. Jean Héder Petit-Frère does not approach this subject as a provocateur, nor as a defender of extremes. He approaches it as a shepherd, with theological depth and pastoral honesty, addressing not money first but lordship, identity, and trust.

This book courageously names the tension many believers feel but cannot articulate: we belong to a rich Kingdom, yet too often live as anxious ambassadors. Rather than offering techniques or transactional promises, Dr. Petit-Frère invites readers into something far more transformative: presence before principles, sonship before stewardship, alignment before increase.

What makes this work particularly compelling is its balance. It neither romanticizes lack nor idolizes abundance. Instead, it restores God as Source and repositions money as a servant exactly where Scripture places it.

This is not a book to be rushed.

It is one to be read prayerfully, honestly, and deliberately.

If you allow its message to do its work, you will not merely change how you think about finances; you will change how you live in the Kingdom.

I wholeheartedly commend this book and the voice behind it.

It is timely.

It is corrective.

And it is deeply needed.

Introduction

Why This Book Had to Be Written

There is a question I have carried for many years.

It surfaced quietly at first, then insistently, and eventually became impossible to ignore. I encountered it in conversations with sincere believers, faithful servants, committed leaders, and generous givers, people who loved God deeply and desired to honor Him sincerely.

The question was simple, yet unsettling:

Why do so many citizens of a rich Kingdom live as though provision were uncertain, peace fragile, and the future insecure?

This book was born from that tension.

We proclaim a Kingdom without lack, yet many believers live under financial pressure.

We declare God as Father, yet anxiety often governs our decisions.

We preach faith, yet fear quietly shapes our expectations.

Something is not right.

This is not an accusation against the Church, nor is it a critique of generosity, discipline, or devotion. On the contrary, this book assumes sincerity. It assumes faith. It assumes a hunger for God.

What it questions is alignment.

Jesus did not announce a poor Kingdom. He proclaimed a Kingdom governed by a loving Father, sustained by divine provision, and accessed through trust rather than toil. When He said, "Seek first the Kingdom of God," He was not offering a poetic ideal. He was revealing a way of life, one where order precedes provision and identity governs experience.

Yet somewhere along the way, many believers learned how to believe without learning how to rest; how to give without learning how to trust; how to work hard without learning how to live from sonship.

This book exists to address that gap.

What This Book Is and What It Is Not

This is not a book about getting rich. It is not a manual on financial techniques. It is not a defense of excess, nor a condemnation of struggle.

This is a book about the Kingdom order.

It is about restoring God as Source, not merely as Helper. It is about dismantling the subtle influence of mammon, not demonizing money.
It is about moving from orphan thinking to sonship security. It is about learning to live in the river where provision flows from presence and peace replaces pressure.

You will not find formulas here. You will find realignment. You will not be given promises to chase. You will be invited into a posture to maintain.

Why Finances Reveal the Heart

Few areas of life expose our beliefs as clearly as money.

How we think about provision reveals how we see God. How we handle resources exposes where we find security.

How we respond to lack or abundance uncovers what truly governs us.

That is why Jesus spoke so often about money, not because it mattered most, but because it revealed what mattered most.

This book approaches finances not as a goal, but as a diagnostic. It asks uncomfortable but necessary questions:

- Who is truly my source?
- What governs my peace?
- Where do fear and control still operate?
- Do I live as a son or as a survivor?

These questions are not meant to condemn. They are meant to be free.

An Invitation, Not an Accusation

If at any point you feel confronted while reading, pause, but do not retreat. Confrontation is often the doorway to clarity. This book does not shame the reader; it entrusts the reader.

The subtitle says it plainly: **Now you hold the cure.**

Not because you generate it, but because you are an ambassador. And ambassadors do not merely announce solutions, they carry them.

The Kingdom does not lack provision. What it requires are aligned representatives.

How to Read This Book

Read slowly.

Reflect honestly.

Resist the urge to skim.

This is not a book to rush through, but a book to walk with. Allow the Scriptures to speak, the questions to surface, and the realignment to take place.

You may find that your circumstances do not change immediately, but your posture will. And posture, in the Kingdom, determines flow.

A Final Word Before We Begin

You were never meant to strive for what your Father already promised.
You were never meant to fear what Christ already secured. You were never meant to survive in a Kingdom designed for abundance.

Something was not right.

This book exists to help restore what was always meant to be.

Let us begin.

Contents

Chapter 1
A Rich King And A Poor Narrative

If the Kingdom you belong to is rich, then poverty cannot be its culture.

Scripture is clear:

"The earth is the Lord's, and the fullness thereof." (Psalm 24:1)

God does not suffer from scarcity.

He does not ration provision.

He does not struggle to meet needs.

And yet, many believers live as though heaven is barely getting by.

This contradiction is not rooted in God's ability; it is rooted in belief systems.

The First Problem: We Start in the Wrong Place

Most financial teaching begins with giving.

"Give, and it shall be given unto you."

That verse is true, but misplaced.

God is far more concerned with your view of money and your heart posture than the amount you give. Giving without alignment does not produce freedom; it often produces frustration.

Financial teaching is powerful because it exposes everything:

- How you see God
- What you believe about provision
- Whether you live as a servant, a son, or an orphan
- Where your sense of security truly comes from

This is why Jesus didn't begin by teaching people how to give. He began by teaching them who the Father is.

The Whole Gospel, Not a Fragmented One

God does not offer partial salvation.

He does not say, "I want you spiritually well but financially stressed."

Jesus paid for the whole package.

"God is able to make all grace, every favor, and earthly blessing come to you in abundance…" (2 Corinthians 9:8, AMP)

Abundance is not excess for the ego.

It is sufficient with margins enough for your needs and enough to bless others.

This does not mean every believer must be a millionaire. It means every believer must be free from lack-driven fear.

Some are specifically called to steward wealth.

Others are called to steward influence, creativity, service, or leadership.

But no one is called to live under bondage.

Poverty Is Not Spiritual

The statement, "I just want enough for myself and my family," sounds humble, but it is often fear that wears religious clothing.

Poverty is not spiritual.

Scarcity is not holiness.

Limitation is not a virtue.

There is a world in need, and God intends to fund His purposes through His people.

"A good man leaves an inheritance to his children's children." (Proverbs 13:22)

Inheritance thinking requires abundance thinking.

And abundance thinking requires Kingdom alignment.

The Hidden Blocker: Traditions That Neutralize Truth

Jesus warned us:

"You make the word of God of no effect through your tradition." (Mark 7:13)

Religious traditions can cancel Kingdom realities not by denying Scripture, but by misframing it.

We have inherited doctrines that:

- Glorify lack
- Spiritualize anxiety
- Distrust prosperity

- Confuse humility with deprivation

This book exists to dismantle those traditions, not to criticize people, but to restore truth.

The Goal of This Journey

We are not chasing money.

We are reclaiming order.

When God is restored as Source, money returns to its proper role as a servant.

When the Kingdom comes first:

- Anxiety loses its grip
- Provision becomes natural
- Giving becomes joyful
- Stewardship becomes effortless
- Abundance becomes purposeful

This chapter is not the solution; it is the doorway.

In the next chapters, we will confront the spirit of mammon, redefine worship, restore sonship, and teach you how to place your finances in the river of God, where multiplication replaces manipulation.

Something was not right.

Now, the Kingdom will restore it.

Pause & Align (End-of-Chapter Reflection)

- Who has truly been my source?
- Where do I feel the most financial anxiety?
- What belief about God might need realignment?

Chapter 2
Mammon: The Rival God Few Recognize

Jesus did not warn us about money.

He warned us about mammon.

"No one can serve two masters… You cannot serve both God and mammon." (Matthew 6:24)

Notice what Jesus did not say.

He did not say, "It will be difficult."

He did not say, "Be careful."

He said, "It is impossible."

This means that many sincere believers are not struggling with finances because they lack faith, but because they are unknowingly serving the wrong master.

Mammon Is Not Money

Money is neutral.

Mammon is spiritual.

Historically, mammon referred to wealth entrusted to a system. Over time, it came to mean confidence placed in riches. By Jesus' day, mammon was recognized as a spiritual power, a rival influence that promises security, identity, and peace apart from God.

Mammon says:

- "If you have enough money, you'll be safe."
- "If your account grows, your value grows."
- "If you lose money, you lose control."

God says:

- "I am your source."
- "I am your security."
- "I freely give you all things."

Mammon does not deny God; it replaces Him quietly.

How Mammon Reveals Itself

Mammon rarely announces itself.

It disguises itself through worry, fear, and control.

Jesus connects mammon directly to anxiety:

"For this reason I tell you, do not worry…" (Matthew 6:25)

Worry is not a personality trait.

Worry is worship.

When you worry about money, you are declaring:

- Money is my protector
- Money is my future
- Money determines my peace

This is why Jesus said that those who worry live like people without a Father.

The Counterfeit Shepherd

Mammon promises what only God can provide.

It whispers:

- "Money is your shepherd."
- "Money will make you lie down in peace."
- "Money will protect you in crisis."

But mammon never satisfies.

It only demands more.

Greed and fear are not opposites; they are twins.

One says, "I don't have enough."

The other says, "I must have more."

Both say, "God is not enough."

Why This Must Be Exposed Before Provision Flows

Many believers give faithfully yet remain bound. not because giving is wrong, but because their hearts are partnered with mammon.

Giving to get is not generosity.

It is a transaction.

Love gives because God is worthy.

Mammon gives only if a return is guaranteed.

Seed sown in fear grows nothing.

Seed sown in trust multiplies naturally.

The Good News: This Can Be Broken Quickly

Mammon loses power the moment its lie is exposed.

Repentance is not shame; it is realignment.

It is the moment you say:

"What was I thinking? God has always been my source."

And in that moment, you step out of the desert and back into the river.

Points To Ponder

- Where do I feel the most financial fear?
- What makes me feel secure, God or money?
- Do I give from love or from expectation?

Call To Action

This week, identify one financial concern you have been carrying alone.

Verbally surrender it to God and declare Him as Source, not backup.

Declaration

I renounce mammon as my master.

God alone is my source, my security, and my provider.

I choose trust over fear, worship over worry, and the Kingdom orders over financial control.

I step fully into the river of God's provision. Amen.

Chapter 3
Seek First The Kingdom, But How?

Few verses are quoted more confidently and practiced more vaguely than this one:

"Seek first the Kingdom of God and His righteousness, and all these things shall be added to you." (Matthew 6:33)

Most believers believe this verse.

Few believers know how to live it.

The issue is not rebellion.

It is a lack of instruction.

Jesus never meant this statement to be poetic comfort. It was a practical strategy for daily life, including finances.

What "Seek First" Does Not Mean

Seeking the Kingdom first does not mean:

- Ignoring responsibilities
- Waiting passively for miracles
- Refusing to plan or work
- Being careless with money and calling it faith

Jesus did not rebuke planningHe rebuked anxious independence.

The Kingdom does not remove responsibility.

It reorders it.

The Context We Often Skip

Matthew 6 is not primarily about money.

It is about lordship.

Jesus contrasts two ways of living:

- A life governed by worry
- A life governed by trust

He does not say unbelievers worry because they are immoral. He says they worry because they have no revelation of the Father.

When believers worry, they are not being sinful; they are being misaligned.

The Core Question Behind The Command

Jesus is asking one fundamental question:

Who determines your priorities, fear or the Father?

To seek the Kingdom first means:

- God defines success
- God determines timing
- God governs provision
- God sets direction

Everything else becomes secondary, not unimportant.

Righteousness Before Resources

Jesus adds something crucial:

"…and His righteousness."

Righteousness is not moral perfection.

It is right-aligned.

To seek righteousness is to bring:

- Your thinking
- Your decisions
- Your finances
- Your expectations

into agreement with who God is and how He operates.

Provision flows most freely where alignment is established.

The Shift From Control To Trust

Seeking the Kingdom first begins when you stop asking:

"How am I going to make this work?"

and start asking:

"God, how do You want to work through this?"

This is the moment finances move from:

- Ownership → Stewardship
- Pressure → Partnership
- Anxiety → Authority

You are no longer trying to force outcomes.

You are cooperating with a higher order.

The Baby on the Father's Lap

Jesus invites us into a picture most adults resist.

A baby does not seek provision.

The baby seeks presence.

Provision follows automatically.

The baby's security is not in planning; it is in the relationship.

This is not irresponsibility.

This is sonship.

Jesus lived this way.

That is why He slept in storms, walked through threats, and never panicked over provision.

What Seeking The Kingdom First Looks Like Practically

It means:

- You bring financial decisions into prayer before panic
- You involve God before stress escalates
- You refuse to make fear-based decisions
- You act from peace, not pressure
- You work diligently, but never independently

Seeking first is not a moment.

It is a posture.

Added Things Follow Ordered Lives

Jesus never said, "Chase provision."

He said, "Align priorities."

When the Kingdom is first:

- Provision becomes added
- Peace becomes normal
- Clarity replaces confusion
- Opportunities appear unexpectedly
- Resources find you

This is not mystical.

It is Kingdom law.

Points To Ponder

- What currently determines my financial decisions?
- Where do I feel the most pressure to "figure it out myself"?
- Have I confused responsibility with control?

Call To Action

This week, before making any financial decision, pause and pray:

"Father, how does Your Kingdom want to express itself here?"

Then act only from peace, not urgency.

Declaration

I seek the Kingdom first, not out of obligation, but out of trust. God orders my steps, governs my resources, and supplies my needs. I refuse anxiety as a guide, and peace is my compass. Provision follows alignment, and I walk in Kingdom order.

Amen.

Chapter 4
God As Source, Money As Servant

Freedom begins the moment you correctly identify your source.

Most financial stress does not come from a lack of money. It comes from misplaced dependency.

When money becomes the source, peace becomes fragile. When God is the source, peace becomes stable regardless of numbers.

Source vs. Resource

A source is original, unchanging, and self-sustaining.

A resource is a channel, temporary, replaceable, and movable.

God is your source.

Your job, business, salary, clients, commissions, investments-these are resources.

This distinction changes everything.

If your job is your source:

- Losing it feels like losing life
- Fear dictates decisions
- Compromise becomes tempting
- Rest disappears

If God is your source:

- Resources may change, but provision does not
- You remain calm in transition

- You move with discernment, not desperation
- Peace governs your steps

Scripture confirms this posture:

"My God shall supply all your need according to His riches in glory." (Philippians 4:19)

Notice where supply comes from, not employment, not systems, not economies, but God's riches.

Why God Allows Resources to Change

Many believers panic when a stream dries up.

But God often changes the place of provision to protect our understanding of the Source.

Elijah was fed by ravens, then by a widow.

The source never changed.

Only the channel did.

When a resource shifts, it is not punishment; it is repositioning.

Money Makes a Poor Master

Money is a terrible god.

It cannot:

- Love you
- Guide you
- Heal you
- Redeem you
- Secure your future

Yet many look to money for what only God provides.

This is why Jesus did not say money was evil. He said serving it was impossible to reconcile with serving God.

Money was designed to be a servant, not a shepherd.

The Moment of Transfer

True freedom comes when you can say without fear:

"God, this belongs to You."

Not just offerings.

Not just tithes.

But:

- Income
- Expenses
- Debts
- Assets
- Dreams
- Responsibilities

This is not surrender to loss.

It is a surrender to multiplication.

The boy's lunch did not become miraculous until it left his hands and entered Jesus' hands.

What remains in your control stays limited.

What enters God's hands becomes expandable.

From Ownership to Stewardship

Ownership says, "This is mine."

Stewardship says, "This has been entrusted to me."

Stewards don't panic.

They manage with confidence because responsibility is shared.

God funds what He governs.

But he only governs what is surrendered.

Why Anxiety Loses Authority Here

Anxiety thrives where control is assumed.

Peace thrives where trust is established.

When God is the source:

- You stop rehearsing worst-case scenarios
- You stop making fear-based compromises
- You stop chasing security
- You start cooperating with heaven

This is not passivity.

It is confidence without strain.

Points To Ponder

- What do I subconsciously treat as my source?
- How do I respond when a resource feels threatened?
- What area of my finances have I not fully surrendered?

Call To Action

Verbally declare out loud, if possible:

"God, You are my source. Every resource in my life is under Your care."

Repeat this daily for the next seven days.

Declaration

God is my source, and I lack nothing.

Money serves the Kingdom in my life; it does not rule it.

I steward resources with wisdom, peace, and trust.

My provision is secure because my source is eternal.

Amen.

Chapter 5
From Orphan Thinking To Sonship Security

Most financial problems are not economic.

They are identity-based.

Two people can earn the same income, give the same amount, attend the same church, and live with completely different levels of peace. The difference is not discipline. It is sonship.

The Orphan Mindset

An orphan mindset says:

- "I am on my own."
- "If I don't protect myself, no one will."
- "Provision depends on my performance."
- "If I fail, I fall."

This mindset produces:

- Anxiety
- Overwork
- Control
- Fear of loss
- Hoarding or striving

Many believers love God sincerely, yet live internally as spiritual orphans.

They believe God is good.

but not reliably involved.

The Sonship Reality

A son does not deny responsibility.

A son denies abandonment.

Jesus lived in absolute awareness of the Father's care.

"The Son can do nothing by Himself, unless it is something He sees the Father doing." (John 5:19)

Jesus never panicked about money.

He never chased provisions.

He never worried about tomorrow.

Why?

Because he knew who was responsible for Him.

Inheritance Changes Everything

Inheritance is not earned.

It is received.

"If children, then heirs of God and joint heirs with Christ." (Romans 8:17)

Imagine discovering that an inheritance was secured for you before you were born. The proper response would not be fear-driven performance, but grateful stewardship.

Religion says, "Behave so God will bless you."

Sonship says, "Because I am blessed, I now learn how to steward."

God does not relate to you based on your performance. He relates to you based on Jesus' performance.

This is not a license.

This is rest.

Why Orphans Struggle With Money

Orphans believe:

- Security must be stored
- Control must be maintained
- Loss must be prevented at all costs

Sons believe:

- Provision flows from a relationship
- Wisdom comes with trust
- God is actively involved

This is why two people can tithe for years and have different outcomes. One gives as an orphan trying to secure favor. The other gives as a son responding to love.

The Baby on the Father's Lap

A baby does not analyze provision.

The baby rests.

The baby's peace is not ignorance; it is trust.

Jesus invites us into that posture:

- Not careless
- Not passive
- But deeply secure

This is the security that silences financial fear.

How Sonship Heals Scarcity

When sonship becomes real:

- Worry loses its authority
- Comparison stops
- Jealousy fades
- Peace stabilizes decisions
- Generosity becomes natural

You stop asking:

"What if I don't have enough?"

And start declaring:

"My Father knows what I need."

Points To Ponder

- Do I relate to God more as a worker or a son?
- How do I respond internally when finances feel threatened?
- Where might orphan thinking still influence my decisions?

Call To Action

Each morning this week, say:

"Father, I trust You with my provision today."

Pause and sit with that truth for one full minute.

Declaration

I am not an orphan. I am a son.

My Father knows my needs and delights in providing for me.

I live from inheritance, not insecurity.

I steward resources with peace, wisdom, and trust.

Amen.

Chapter 6
Worship, Worth, and What You Serve

Every life is organized around something.

That "something" becomes the plumb line, the standard by which decisions are made, risks are taken, and priorities are set.

Scripture calls this worship.

Worship is not primarily what happens on a stage.

Worship is what you ascribe worth to.

What Worship Really Is

The word *worship* comes from *worth-ship*to assign value, weight, and authority to someone or something.

To worship is to say:

- "This matters most."
- "This defines reality for me."
- "This will guide my life."

Jesus tied worship directly to service:

"No one can serve two masters."

Service reveals worship.

Worship reveals lordship.

You don't worship what you sing to; you worship what you organize your life around.

Why Jesus Connected Worship to Money

Money is the most common competitor for ultimate value.

Not because money is evil, but because money offers what only God can give:

- Security
- Control
- Identity
- Peace
- Options

This is why Jesus did not say, "Be careful with money."

He said, "You cannot serve both."

Magnetic North

Every life has a magnetic north.

a fixed point that determines direction.

If money is your magnetic north:

- Peace rises and falls with numbers
- Confidence fluctuates with income
- Fear increases when resources tighten

If God is your magnetic north:

- Peace remains steady
- Decisions flow from trust
- Provision becomes added, not chased

Worship establishes direction before it ever produces provision.

Why Anxiety Is a Worship Issue

Jesus connects mammon directly to worry.

When you worry about money, you are not being irresponsible; you are placing ultimate value somewhere.

Worry says:

- "This situation is bigger than God."
- "I must figure this out alone."
- "Provision depends on me."

That is worship misdirected.

Peace is not denial.

Peace is confidence in who governs the outcome.

The Plumb Line Illustration

A plumb line determines what is straight.

If the plumb line is off, everything built on it will not matter, no matter how sincere the builder.

Jesus Himself is the plumb line.

He revealed a Father who:

- Loves unconditionally
- Provides faithfully
- Governs wisely
- Invites trust fully

When worship is realigned, finances follow naturally.

Worship Orders Life

Worship is saying:

"God, You are the highest value in my life."

And then ordering:

- Spending
- Saving
- Giving
- Working
- Resting

around that truth.

This is why Jesus said:

"Seek first the Kingdom..."

First is not a position; it is a priority.

The Result of Right Worship

When worship is rightly placed:

- Fear loses influence
- Greed loses appeal
- Generosity brings joy
- Stewardship becomes natural
- Provision accelerates quietly

Money begins to serve rather than dominate.

Points To Ponder

- What do I instinctively turn to for security?
- What determines my sense of peace?
- What do my financial decisions reveal about my worship?

Call To Action

This week, before spending or stressing, ask:

"Does this decision reflect what I truly value?"

Let worship, not urgency, guide your choices.

Declaration

God alone is worthy of my highest devotion.

I order my life around His truth, His care, and His Kingdom.

Money serves God's purpose in my life; it does not rule it.

I live aligned, anchored, and free.

Amen.

Chapter 7
The River and the Desert

There are two environments in which people attempt to live their financial lives:

the desert and the river.

Both are real.

Only one produces life.

The Desert of Striving

The desert is where many believers unknowingly live.

It is dry not because God is absent, but because everything depends on human effort.

In the desert:

- You pray, but still panic
- You work hard, but feel alone
- You give, but feel pressure
- You plan, but lack peace

The desert mentality says:

"If I don't figure this out, no one will."

This is not rebellion; it is self-reliance born from fear.

The tragedy is that many call this responsibility, when in fact it is separation.

The River of the Kingdom

Jesus did not invite us into a system.

He invited us into a flow.

Scripture consistently describes God's life as a river:

- A river that heals (Ezekiel 47)
- A river that satisfies (Psalm 46)
- A river of living water (John 7:38)

A river is not static.

It moves, carries, nourishes, and influences everything within it.

What Happens When You Enter a River

When you step into a river:

- You come under its influence
- You are no longer stationary
- You are carried in a direction
- You are affected by its current

Anything placed in the river becomes subject to the flow.

This is the Kingdom principle many miss.

When you place your finances in the river of God's Kingdom, they are no longer governed by fear, pressure, or limitation. They become available for divine influence.

Why Many Pray but Stay Dry

Many believers pray to God while keeping their finances outside the river.

They say:

- "God, bless this."
- "God, help me."
- "God, fix this."

But they never release control.

They are trying to swim in a desert.

Prayer without surrender keeps you dry.

Surrender places you in the flow.

The Lunch That Became a Miracle

The boy with five loaves and two fish was not making an offering.
He was carrying lunch.

It was ordinary.

Limited.

Insufficient.

But once it entered Jesus' hands, the natural became supernatural.

Nothing multiplied until it was released.

What you hold onto remains what it is.

What you release becomes what God makes it.

Putting Finances in the River

Putting your finances in the river does not mean irresponsibility. It means invitation.

You are saying:

"God, this belongs to You.

Influence it. Direct it. Multiply it."

This is where provision accelerates, not through pressure, but through presence.

Rest Is a River Skill

You cannot rest in the desert.

Rest only works where trust is established.

In the river:

- You still work, but without panic
- You still plan, but without fear
- You still steward, but without anxiety

Rest is not inactivity.

It is confidence in governance.

Why Flow Feels Unfamiliar

Many believers resist the river because:

- Control feels safer than trust
- Familiar stress feels normal

- Peace feels irresponsible

But the Kingdom operates by trust, not tension.

Jesus slept in storms not because He ignored reality, but because He knew who governed it.

Points To Ponder

- Where am I striving instead of trusting?
- What area of my finances have I kept outside the river?
- What would change if I truly believed God was involved?

Call To Action

Take one financial concern you've been carrying and say aloud:

"God, I place this in Your river."

Refuse to rehearse fear about it afterward.

Declaration

I step out of striving and into the river of God.

My finances are under Kingdom influence.

God directs, supplies, and multiplies what I surrender.

I live carried, not pressured, at rest, not in fear.

Amen.

Chapter 8
Putting Your Finances In The River

Understanding the river is powerful.

Entering it is transformative.

Many believers agree with Kingdom truth intellectually, yet continue to live financially unchanged, not because they don't believe, but because they don't know how to transfer ownership in real life.

Putting your finances in the river is not mystical.

It is intentional, relational, and practical.

Step One: Acknowledge Ownership Transfer

The river begins with a clear decision:

"God, this is no longer mine; it is entrusted to me."

This is not symbolic language.

It is a governance shift.

Until ownership is addressed, anxiety remains justified because you still believe everything depends on you.

Stewardship begins where ownership ends.

Step Two: Invite God Before You React

Most people invite God after panic begins.

Kingdom living invites God before pressure escalates.

Putting finances in the river means:

- You pray before stressing
- You pause before deciding
- You ask before acting
- You listen before controlling

This slows nothing down.

It actually accelerates clarity.

Step Three: Refuse Fear-Based Decisions

Fear always demands immediacy.

Peace invites discernment.

Not every financial opportunity is a Kingdom provision. Not every urgent situation requires rushed action.

The river teaches you to move with God, not ahead of Him.

If peace leaves, pause.

Peace is not a feeling; it is a governing signal.

Step Four: Give as an Act of Trust, Not Transaction

Giving does not put finances in the river.

Trust does.

Giving without trust is still desert living.

When you give:

- Not to get
- Not to impress
- Not to secure
- But to honor

…you are declaring God as Source.

God gives seed to sowers, not gamblers.

Step Five: Work Without Anxiety

Putting finances in the river does not remove diligence. It removes pressure.

You still:

- Budget
- Plan
- Save
- Work
- Invest
- Learn

But now you do so:

- Without panic
- Without fear of loss
- Without obsession
- Without self-protection

You are working with heaven, not competing against time.

Step Six: Expect God's Involvement

Many believers surrender but do not expect.

Expectation is faith's posture.

When finances are in the river, you begin to say:

- "God, show me."
- "God, redirect me."
- "God, surprise me."

And He does often through:

- Ideas
- Favor
- Connections
- Timing
- Wisdom
- Opportunity

Provision rarely falls from the sky.

It usually flows through obedient alignment.

When the River Tests You

There will be moments when:

- Resources tighten
- Answers delay
- Faith stretches

The river is not the absence of challenge.

It is present in the challenge.

You do not exit the river when pressure rises; you go deeper.

Points To Ponder

- Where do I react instead of invite?
- What financial decisions have I made under fear?
- Do I truly expect God to be involved daily?

Call To Action

This week, practice the pause.

Before every financial action, pause for ten seconds and acknowledge God as Source.

Declaration

My finances are in the river of God.

I steward with wisdom, act with peace, and trust without fear.

God directs my steps and multiplies what I surrender.

I live under Kingdom influence daily.

Amen.

Chapter 9
Abundance Without Guilt Or Greed

Few words have been more misunderstood, abused, or feared in the Church than the word *prosperity*.

Some reject it out of conviction.

Others pursue it out of ambition.

Many are simply confused.

The problem is not the word; it is the framework in which it has been taught.

Why Abundance Triggers Resistance

When finances are mentioned, reactions surface quickly:

- Suspicion
- Defensiveness
- Guilt
- Cynicism

Not because abundance is unbiblical, but because it has often been presented:

- Without presence
- Without process
- Without character
- Without purpose

Abuse does not nullify truth.

It calls for restoration, not rejection.

Biblical Abundance Defined

Abundance is not excess for self-indulgence.

It is sufficient with a margin.

Scripture describes it clearly:

"God is able to make all grace abound toward you, that you, always having all sufficiency in all things, may have an abundance for every good work." (2 Corinthians 9:8)

Notice the progression:

1. Sufficiency for your needs
2. Margin for generosity
3. Capacity for Kingdom impact

Abundance is not about luxury.

It is about availability.

Why Poverty Is Not a Virtue

Poverty is not humility.

Lack is not holiness.

Struggle is not sanctification.

Poverty limits reach, compresses vision, and restricts generosity.

God does not glorify lack. He redeems people from it.

Jesus never celebrated scarcity.

He addressed the need with a provision.

Why Greed Is Not Abundance

Greed is abundance without governance.

It is accumulation without alignment, increase without intimacy, and gain without gratitude.

Greed says:

- "More will satisfy me."

Abundance says:

- "God satisfies me; therefore, I steward more."

One is rooted in insecurity.

The other is rooted in rest.

Abundance Under Grace

Under grace, God does not increase resources to test obedience. He increases his capacity to fulfill the assignment.

Provision follows purpose.

Some are called to steward significant wealth.

Others are called to steward influence, skill, leadership, creativity, or service.

But no one is called to live bound by fear of lack.

Why Many Never Step Into Abundance

Because abundance requires:

- Trust without anxiety
- Stewardship without control
- Giving without manipulation
- Receiving without guilt

Many believers sabotage the increase because they:

- Feel unworthy
- Fear judgment
- Associate abundance with pride
- Confuse humility with limitation

The Kingdom does not reward shame.

It responds to alignment.

The Whole-Package Gospel

God does not choose between spiritual and material well-being.

He restores:

- Spirit
- Soul
- Body
- Relationships
- Purpose
- Provision

A fragmented gospel produces fractured believers. A whole gospel produces whole lives.

Points To Ponder

- What emotions surface when I think about abundance?
- Have I associated prosperity with guilt or greed?
- Do I believe God delights in my provision?

Call To Action

Ask God this question in prayer:

"Father, what is your definition of abundance for my life?"

Write down what He reveals without editing it.

Declaration

I receive God's provision without guilt and steward it without greed.

Abundance flows through alignment, not ambition.

I have enough for my needs and a margin for God's purposes.

My life reflects Kingdom wholeness.

Amen.

Chapter 10
Giving Under Grace, Not Pressure

Giving has been one of the most misunderstood spiritual practices in the lives of believers, not because Scripture is unclear, but because motivation has often been distorted.

Many people give faithfully, yet joylessly.

Others give generously, yet anxiously.

Some stop giving altogether, not out of rebellion, but out of fatigue and confusion.

This chapter exists to restore giving to its rightful place, not as a lever to move God, but as a response to Him.

The Problem with Transactional Giving

Transactional giving sounds spiritual, but it is rooted in fear.

It says:

- "If I give, God will bless me."
- "If I sow, I will secure a return."
- "If I let this go, I must make sure it comes back."

This posture turns giving into a contract, not worship.

Grace does not function on exchange.

Grace functions on relationships.

When giving is driven by fear of lack or hope of gain, it no longer reflects trust; it reflects self-protection.

What Grace Changes About Giving

Under grace, God is not responding to your generosity He is revealing His nature.

"He who did not spare His own Son, but delivered Him up for us all, how shall He not also with Him freely give us all things?" (Romans 8:32)

Giving under grace begins with this conviction:

God has already proven His willingness to provide.

Therefore, giving is no longer:

- A means to provoke blessing
- A way to earn favor
- A test of worthiness

It becomes an expression of trust and alignment.

Seed, Sower, and Source

Scripture says God gives seed to the sower.

That statement reveals three things:

1. God is the source
2. You are the steward
3. Giving is directional, not random

God does not fund fear-based sowing.

He funds a faith-filled partnership.

When the heart is aligned, return is not forced; it is natural.

Why Pressure Cancels Grace

Pressure creates resistance.

Grace creates a response.

When people are manipulated into giving:

- Hearts close
- Joy disappears
- Fear increases
- Trust erodes

God does not need coercion to fund His Kingdom.

He desires willing participation.

"God loves a cheerful giver." (2 Corinthians 9:7)

Cheerfulness is not an emotion; it is freedom from fear.

Giving as Worship

True giving is an act of worship.

It says:

"God, You are my source.

This provision came from You, and it returns to You."

Worship is never anxious.

Worship is never rushed.

Worship is never manipulative.

When giving becomes worship, money loses its grip and generosity flows without strain.

When Giving Is Misunderstood

Some believers stop giving because they were wounded by misuse.
Others continue giving but remain internally conflicted.

The answer is not to abandon giving.

It is to restore understanding.

Giving under grace is:

- Voluntary
- Joyful
- Purposeful
- Peaceful
- Trust-based

It is not about the amount.

It is about alignment.

Points To Ponder

- What has motivated my giving in the past?
- Have I ever given in out of fear or pressure?
- Do I view giving as worship or transaction?

Call To Action

The next time you give, whether money, time, or a resource, pause and say:

"Father, I give this freely, trusting You completely."

Declaration

I give under grace, not pressure.

My generosity flows from trust, not fear.

God is my source, and I partner with Him joyfully.

I give freely, steward wisely, and live confidently.

Amen.

Chapter 11
Stewardship Without Anxiety

Stewardship was never meant to be stressful.

Yet for many believers, managing money feels like walking a tightrope, one misstep away from collapse. Budgets create tension. Planning creates pressure. Responsibility feels heavy.

This was never God's design.

Anxiety does not improve stewardship.

It distorts it.

What Stewardship Really Is

Stewardship is not ownership with extra rules.

It is management with shared responsibility.

A steward does not fund the vision.

The owner does.

The steward:

- Manages resources
- Follows direction
- Acts faithfully
- Reports honestly

The weight of the outcome never rests on the steward alone.

When stewardship becomes anxious, it usually means ownership has quietly crept back in.

Why Anxiety Feels Responsible but Isn't

Anxiety often masquerades as wisdom.

People say:

- "I'm just being careful."
- "I'm just thinking ahead."
- "I'm just trying to be responsible."

But anxiety does not come from foresight.

It comes from the fear of being alone.

Jesus addressed this directly:

"Which of you, by worrying, can add one cubit to his stature?" (Matthew 6:27)

Worry adds nothing.

It only drains clarity.

Peace Is a Stewardship Tool

Peace is not the absence of responsibility.

It is the presence of trust.

Peace allows you to:

- See clearly
- Decide wisely
- Wait patiently
- Act courageously
- Adjust without panic

An anxious mind rushes.

A peaceful mind listens.

Planning with God, Not Instead of God

Kingdom stewardship still plans, but never independently.

Your budget.

You save.

You invest.

You prepare.

But you do so:

- With prayer
- With flexibility
- With listening
- With expectation

Plans are not prisons.

They are frameworks for obedience.

When God redirects, peaceful stewards adjust without an identity crisis.

Why Stewardship Thrives in the River

In the river:

- You manage without obsession
- You plan without fear
- You steward without hoarding
- You release without panic

You know:

- God sees what you don't
- God supplies what you lack
- God redirects when needed

Stewardship becomes cooperative, not burdensome.

When Resources Feel Tight

Tight seasons do not mean failure.

They mean attention.

Instead of panic, ask:

- "God, what are You teaching me?"
- "What needs refining?"
- "Where do I need wisdom?"

God often trains stewards in restraint before entrusting increase.

Faithful with Little, Free with Much

Jesus said faithfulness precedes increase, not stress.

Faithful stewardship:

- Honors God
- Serves a purpose
- Respects process
- Maintains peace

Increase does not reward pressure.

It responds to trustworthy alignment.

Points To Ponder

- Where does anxiety show up in my financial planning?
- Do I treat budgets as tools or burdens?
- How do I respond when plans change?

Call To Action

Review your current financial plan this week and pray:

"God, show me where peace needs to replace pressure."

Make one adjustment led by peace, not fear.

Declaration

I steward God's resources with wisdom and peace.

Anxiety does not govern my decisions; trust does.

I plan responsibly, adjust humbly, and rest confidently.

God partners with me in every financial season.

Amen.

Chapter 12
When Worry Becomes Worship

Worry rarely feels spiritual.

Yet Jesus treated it as a theological issue, not an emotional one.

"For this reason I tell you, do not worry…" (Matthew 6:25)

That phrase—*for this reason*—connects worry directly to **who you serve.** Jesus is not merely calming nerves; He is exposing **misplaced devotion.**

Why Worry Is Never Neutral

Worry is not simply concern taken too far.

Worry is attention with allegiance.

When worry dominates, it declares:

- "This problem defines reality."
- "This outcome controls my peace."
- "This situation is bigger than God's care."

That is not logic.

That is worship misdirected.

The Object of Your Focus Governs You

Whatever occupies your mind repeatedly shapes your trust.

Worship works this way:

- You focus

- You value
- You align
- You serve

Worry follows the same pattern.

When worry governs finances, money becomes the measure of:

- Safety
- Identity
- Control
- Future

Jesus calls this serving mammon.

Why Jesus Took Worry Seriously

Jesus did not rebuke people for planning.

He rebuked them for living as though they had no Father.

"These things dominate the thoughts of unbelievers." (Matthew 6:32)

Believers can live like unbelievers, not by rejecting God, but by excluding Him from trust.

Worry is not proof of humility.

It is proof of disconnection.

Two Expressions of the Same Lie

Mammon manifests in two opposite but related ways:

- Fear: "I don't have enough."
- Greed: "I must have more."

Both say the same thing:

"God is not sufficient."

That lie fuels anxiety in the poor and obsession in the wealthy. It does not discriminate by income, only by belief.

How Worry Shapes Decisions

Worry pushes you to:

- Rush decisions
- Compromise values
- Hoard resources
- Overwork
- Resist generosity

It feels productive, but it is reactive.

Faith does not ignore reality.

Faith refuses to let fear interpret it.

Replacing Worry with Worship

Worship does not deny problems.

It reframes authority.

To worship God in the face of financial pressure is to say:

"You are greater than this moment."

This is not passive optimism.

It is active trust.

When worship rises, worry loses ground because only one master can rule at a time.

Practicing the Exchange

When worry surfaces, do not shame yourself.

Recognize it as an invitation.

Ask:

- "What am I trusting right now?"
- "Who am I looking to for security?"
- "What would worship look like in this moment?"

Then respond not with panic, but with alignment.

Points To Ponder

- What financial situations trigger worry most often?
- What does my worry reveal about my trust?
- How might worship reframe this concern?

Call To Action

Each time worry arises this week, pause and speak one sentence of worship aloud, acknowledging God's care and authority over that situation.

Declaration

I refuse to worry as a master.

God alone governs my peace and provision.

I choose worship over anxiety and trust over fear.

My life is ordered by the Kingdom, not by pressure.

Amen.

Chapter 13
Repentance: Changing The Plumb Line

Repentance has suffered from a poor definition.

For many, it means feeling bad, saying sorry, or promising to do better. But biblical repentance is none of those things. It is not emotional regret; it is mental realignment.

The word *repent* means to change the way you think.

Repentance is the moment you realize:

"I've been building straight walls on a crooked standard."

The Power of the Plumb Line

A plumb line establishes what is straight.

If the plumb line is off, every structure, no matter how sincere the effort, will lean.

Many believers are not failing financially because they are disobedient.
They are failing because they are measuring life by the wrong standard.

The Kingdom has a plumb line.

Jesus revealed it.

When the Wrong Standard Governs Life

When money becomes the plumb line:

- Security is measured by savings
- Peace is measured by income
- Identity is measured by success
- Fear rises when resources fluctuate

This does not mean money is evil.

It means it has been asked to do what only God can do.

Repentance is not saying, "I'm sorry for trusting money." It is saying, "Money was never meant to be my reference point."

Jesus as the Ultimate Standard

Jesus did not merely teach truth.

He embodied it.

He revealed a Father who:

- Provides without manipulation
- Guides without pressure
- Corrects without condemnation
- Supplies without scarcity

To repent is to agree with this revelation and reorder life accordingly.

Why Repentance Is Liberating

Repentance removes pressure.

It is the moment you stop trying to fix outcomes and start aligning with the truth.

Instead of asking:

"What did I do wrong?"

You begin asking:

"What am I seeing incorrectly?"

This shift restores peace quickly because peace is the fruit of alignment, not perfection.

Scrapping the Fence

Imagine building a fence, only to realize the foundation is crooked.

You don't apologize to the fence; you rebuild from the right standard.

True repentance says:

"Let's start over from the truth."

God does not shame you for misalignment.

He invites you into clarity

Living from the New Standard

Once the plumb line is corrected:

- Decisions become simpler
- Anxiety loses authority
- Worship becomes natural
- Stewardship becomes light
- Provision follows order

Repentance is not an event.

It is a way of living aligned.

Points To Ponder

- What has been my practical plumb line in financial decisions?
- Where might fear have replaced truth?
- What needs realignment rather than regret?

Call To Action

Write down one belief about money you are releasing and replace it with a Kingdom truth grounded in Scripture.

Declaration

I realign my thinking with Kingdom truth.

Jesus is my plumb line, not money, fear, or pressure.

I build my life on truth, and peace follows naturally.

My steps are ordered, my heart is free, and my provision is secure.

Amen.

Chapter 14
Provision With Purpose

God does not provide randomly.

He provides intentionally.

Provision in the Kingdom is never detached from purpose. When God supplies, He is not merely meeting needs; He is funding assignments.

This is where many misunderstand abundance. They assume provision exists for comfort alone. But comfort is never the goal; impact is.

Why God Funds Purpose, Not Ego

God has no interest in inflating self-importance.

He delights in advancing His Kingdom through willing stewards.

When resources increase without purpose, pride follows. When purpose leads, provision follows.

Jesus never accumulated wealth, yet He never lacked. Why?

Because everything He needed to fulfill His assignment was always available.

Provision is not about lifestyle, it is about obedience.

The Flow of Kingdom Provision

Kingdom provision follows a clear order:

1. Calling reveals assignment
2. Assignment requires provision
3. Provision follows alignment
4. Stewardship multiplies impact

When this order is reversed, when provision is sought without purpose, confusion and frustration arise.

Why Many Stall at "Enough"

Some believers stop believing in God for good once their personal needs are met. It feels humble, but it quietly limits Kingdom's reach.

Enough for survival is not enough for the mission.

The question is not:

"Do I have enough for myself?"

But:

"Do I have enough to do what God has put in my heart?"

God expands capacity where hearts remain outward-facing.

Assignment Clarifies Desire

When the purpose is unclear, money becomes the focus. When purpose is clear, money becomes fuel.

Purpose answers questions like:

- Why do I want to increase?
- Who am I called to serve?
- What problem am I meant to help solve?
- What part of the Kingdom am I meant to advance?

Without purpose, increase creates pressure.

With purpose, increase creates momentum.

Provision Without Pressure

When provision is tied to assignment:

- Comparison fades
- Jealousy loses power
- Fear diminishes
- Contentment grows
- Expectation becomes healthy

You stop measuring your life against others and start measuring it against obedience.

Funding the Will of God

God's will is not abstract.

It expresses itself through:

- People
- Places
- Initiatives
- Solutions
- Restoration
- Compassion
- Justice

And all of these require resources.

God's plan has always been to fund His work through His people, not apart from them.

When Provision Feels Delayed

Delayed provision is often an invitation to:

- Clarify assignment
- Strengthen stewardship
- Refine motives
- Deepen trust

Delay is not denial.

It is often preparation.

Points To Ponder

- What assignments has God placed on my heart?
- Do I see provision as personal comfort or Kingdom fuel?
- Where might the purpose need greater clarity?

Call To Action

Ask God in prayer this week:

"Father, what assignment are you currently funding in my life?"

Write down what comes to mind and revisit it regularly.

Declaration

God provides for His purposes through my life.

I am a steward of Kingdom resources, not a consumer of blessings.

Provision flows to assignment, and I walk in clarity and obedience.

My resources serve God's will, and His will directs my resources.

Amen.

Chapter 15
Inheritance Thinking

Scarcity thinking asks, "Will I have enough?"

Inheritance thinking asks, "What has already been given?"

The difference between these two mindsets determines whether a believer lives cautiously or confidently.

Inheritance thinking is not optimism.

It is theology rightly understood.

Inheritance Is Established Before Effort

An inheritance is not earned.

It is secured by a relationship.

"If children, then heirs of God and joint heirs with Christ." (Romans 8:17)

This means the provision was settled before the performance.

Religion says, "Prove yourself, and you'll be blessed."

The Kingdom says, "You are blessed, now learn how to steward."

This truth dismantles fear at its root.

Why Many Live Beneath Their Inheritance

Many believers believe in inheritance theologically, but not practically.

They believe heaven is guaranteed.

But the provision feels uncertain.

Why?

Because inheritance requires trust in the Giver, not confidence in the self.

Living beneath inheritance often looks like:

- Overworking to feel secure
- Hoarding resources "just in case."
- Fear of generosity
- Anxiety about tomorrow

These are not moral failures.

They are identity gaps.

Inheritance Produces Responsibility, Not Passivity

Inheritance does not remove responsibility; it clarifies it.

If you inherited a vast estate, you would not:

- Ignore it
- Fear it
- Waste it

You would learn:

- How it works

- How to manage it
- How to protect it
- How to multiply it

Inheritance thinking produces dignity, not entitlement.

Living Today from Tomorrow's Certainty

Inheritance thinking allows you to live today with tomorrow settled.

This does not eliminate challenges.

It eliminates panic.

You face uncertainty differently when you know:

- Provision is guaranteed
- Direction is available
- Help is present
- Correction is loving

Inheritance thinking replaces survival mode with stewardship mode.

From Accumulation to Legacy

Scarcity accumulates for safety.

Inheritance is built for legacy.

Legacy thinking asks:

- What will remain?
- Who will benefit?
- What will continue after me?

God's Kingdom always thinks in generations.

"A good man leaves an inheritance to his children's children." (Proverbs 13:22)

Inheritance thinking expands time horizons and with it, faith.

Points To Ponder

- Do I live as a manager or a survivor?
- Where do I fear losing what God has already secured?
- How might inheritance thinking change my decisions?

Call To Action

This week, ask yourself before major decisions:

"Am I acting like someone protecting scarcity or stewarding inheritance?"

Declaration

I live from inheritance, not insecurity.

God has already provided what I need for obedience.

I steward today with confidence in tomorrow's provision.

My life reflects Kingdom legacy.

Amen.

Chapter 16
Money Hunts You Down

This statement unsettles some and excites others.

It should do neither.

It is not a promise of ease.

It is a description of the Kingdom order.

When alignment is complete, provision becomes responsive, not forced.

Provision as a Consequence, Not a Goal

In the Kingdom, money is never the goal.

It is the result of alignment.

When:

- God is the source
- Sonship is secure
- Worship is ordered
- Stewardship is faithful
- Purpose is clear

Provision accelerates quietly.

Opportunities appear.

Ideas emerge.

Favor opens doors.

Connections form.

Not because money is chased

But because the Kingdom is expressed.

Why Provision Finds Aligned People

God entrusts resources where they will:

- Be stewarded wisely
- Serve purpose
- Remain under worship
- Multiply impact

Money flows toward alignment, the way water flows downhill. naturally, predictably, without striving.

When Increase Feels Effortless

Effortless does not mean effortless work.

It means effort without anxiety.

You still show up.

You still labor.

You still learn.

You still adjust.

But stress no longer drives you.

Peace does.

The Danger of Misinterpreting This Truth

This is not a promise of instant wealth.

It is a description of long-term Kingdom fruitfulness.

Some experience immediate breakthroughs.

Others see a steady, sustained increase.

Both are expressions of God's wisdom.

The goal is not speed.

The goal is stability.

Staying Aligned in Seasons of Increase

Increase test alignment.

As resources grow:

- Gratitude must deepen
- Worship must remain central
- Generosity must stay intentional
- Identity must remain rooted

Alignment is not achieved once it is maintained.

Points To Ponder

- Do I chase provision or alignment?
- How do I respond when opportunities increase?
- Is my peace dependent on outcomes?

Call To Action

When provision shows up, large or small, pause to acknowledge God as Source before responding.

Declaration

I walk in Kingdom alignment, and provision responds naturally.

Money serves God's purpose through my life.

I remain rooted in worship, peace, and trust.

My increase is stable, purposeful, and God-governed.

Amen.

Conclusion

Living in the River

The goal of this book was never to teach you how to get money. It was to teach you how to get aligned.

Money was never the real issue.

Fear was.

Identity was.

The order was.

We began with a tension that could no longer be ignored: a rich Kingdom represented by anxious ambassadors.

That contradiction did not exist in the mind of God; it emerged in the thinking of His people.

Jesus did not announce a poor Kingdom.

He announced a Kingdom where sons live under the care of a Father, where provision flows from presence, and where anxiety is replaced by trust.

Yet somewhere along the way, many believers learned how to survive but not how to rest; how to give but not how to trust; how to work, but not how to flow.

This book was written to correct that.

The River Is Not a Concept. It Is a Way of Life

Living in the river does not mean your life becomes effortless. It means your life becomes governed.

In the river:

- God remains your source

- Peace becomes your posture

- Worship becomes your compass

- Stewardship becomes your joy

- Provision becomes responsive

The river represents Kingdom influence, the moment when you stop asking God to bless what you control and start surrendering what He wants to govern.

You were never meant to manage life alone.

The river is what happens when:

- Sonship replaces orphan thinking
- Worship replaces worry
- Trust replaces control
- Alignment replaces striving

It is the environment where God places His Spirit in your nature.

Why Many Step In and Then Step Out

Some believers taste freedom but return to fear.

Not because God failed, but because alignment must be maintained.

Living in the river requires vigilance:

- Guarding your thought life
- Refusing fear-based decisions
- Resisting comparison
- Staying rooted in worship
- Continually realigning your plumb line

The desert is familiar.

The river requires trust.

But once you have tasted peace without pressure, you can no longer pretend anxiety is normal.

Ambassadors Represent the Nature of Their King

An anxious ambassador misrepresents the King.

A fearful ambassador distorts the message.

A striving ambassador obscures the Kingdom.

A rich King deserves ambassadors who:

- Trust deeply
- Rest confidently
- Steward wisely
- Give joyfully
- Live freely

This is not arrogance.

It is accuracy.

When ambassadors live aligned, the Kingdom becomes visible, not just preached.

This Is Not the End. It Is the New Order

This book does not end with a promise of instant breakthrough. It ends with a call to consistency.

Living in the river is not a one-time surrender.

It is a daily posture.

Each day you will choose:

- Fear or faith
- Control or trust
- Worry or worship
- Scarcity or inheritance

And each day, the Kingdom responds not to effort, but to alignment.

Provision follows order.

Peace follows trust.

Abundance follows purpose.

A Final Word

You were never meant to strive for what your Father already promised.

You were never meant to beg for what Christ already purchased.

You were never meant to survive in a Kingdom designed for abundance.

Something was not right.

Now it has been realigned.

Stay in the river.

Remain aligned.

Let worship govern your life.

And let provision follow naturally.

Final Points To Ponder

- Am I living from trust or fear?
- What regularly pulls me out of the river?
- How does my life represent the King I serve?

Final Call To Action

Make a conscious decision today:

"I will no longer live outside Kingdom alignment."

Revisit this book whenever pressure tries to replace peace.

Final Declaration

I live as an ambassador of a rich Kingdom.

God is my source, peace is my posture, and trust is my foundation.

I remain in the river of God's provision and presence.

My life reflects the generosity, care, and abundance of my King.

Amen.

Appendix

A. Kingdom Alignment Prayers

These prayers are not formulas.

They are relational resets meant to be prayed slowly, honestly, and repeatedly.

Prayer 1: Re-establishing God as Source

Father,
I acknowledge You as my only true source.

Forgive me for the times I have looked to money, systems, or people for what only You can provide.

I realign my trust today, not in the provision itself, but in You, the Provider.

Let my heart rest in Your care, and let my life reflect confidence in Your faithfulness.

Amen.

Prayer 2: Releasing Control and Fear

Father,
I release the burden of control.

I confess that fear has often driven my decisions.

Today, I place my finances fully in Your hands.

Teach me to steward without anxiety and to trust without hesitation.

I choose peace over pressure and worship over worry.

Amen.

Prayer 3: Entering the River

Father,
I step out of striving and into Your river.

I bring my income, my responsibilities, my debts, my dreams, and my future under Your influence.

Let Your wisdom guide me, Your presence lead me, and Your provision flow freely.

I trust You to place Your super on my natural.

Amen.

B. Declarations for Financial Freedom

Speak these declarations regularly, especially when fear, pressure, or uncertainty arise:

- God is my source; I lack nothing.
- I live as a son, not an orphan.
- Money serves the Kingdom in my life; it does not rule it.
- I steward resources with wisdom, peace, and joy.
- I refuse anxiety as a guide; peace governs my decisions.
- Provision follows alignment, not striving.
- I live in the river of God's Kingdom.
- My life reflects trust, abundance, and purpose.

C. Ongoing Heart-Check Questions

Return to these questions monthly or whenever financial pressure increases:

1.   What is currently shaping my sense of security?

2.   Am I responding to this situation from peace or fear?

3.   Have I invited God into this decision, or only informed Him afterward?

4.   Is my giving flowing from love or obligation?

5.   Am I stewarding from inheritance or scarcity?

6.   What would worship look like in this situation?

7.   Where might I need to realign my plumb line?

D. A Final Charge to the Reader

You were never meant to survive the Kingdom. You were called to represent it.

A rich King deserves ambassadors who:

- Trust deeply
- Live freely
- Give joyfully
- Steward wisely
- Walk peacefully

This book is not the end of a journey.

It is the correction of direction.

Stay in the river.

Remain aligned.

Let worship govern your life.

And let provision follow naturally.

Final Declaration

I live as an ambassador of a rich Kingdom.

God is my source, peace is my posture, and trust is my foundation.

I steward abundance with humility and purpose.

My life reflects the generosity, provision, and care of my Father.

Amen.

Author Bio

Dr. Jean Héder Petit-Frère is a pastor, teacher, author, and global Kingdom voice with over three decades of ministry experience. Known for his depth, clarity, and uncompromising commitment to biblical truth, he has dedicated his life to helping believers discover their identity as sons and daughters of God and live fully aligned with Kingdom realities.

As the founder and leader of multiple ministries and educational initiatives, Dr. Petit-Frère has served communities across Haiti, North America, and the French-speaking world, equipping leaders, families, and institutions for spiritual, social, and generational transformation.

A prolific author, Dr. Petit-Frère writes at the intersection of theology, identity, leadership, and practical Kingdom living. His teachings challenge religious mindsets while restoring confidence in God's goodness, provision, and purpose.

He lives and ministers with a clear conviction:

A rich King deserves confident ambassadors.

www.ingramcontent.com/pod-product-compliance
Lightning Source LLC
Chambersburg PA
CBHW061745050726
47598CB00002B/596